VALLEJO CITY UNIFIED SCHOOL DISTRICT
PENNYCOOK 45-15 YEAR ROUND SCHOOL
3620 SHERWOOD STREET
VALLEJO CALIFORNIA 94590
PHONE 643-8241

YOUR HEALTH

Health and Friends

Dorothy Baldwin

Rourke Enterprises, Inc.
Vero Beach, FL, 32964

Your Health

Health and Food
Health and Exercise
Health and Drugs
Health and Hygiene
Health and Feelings
Health and Friends

Some words in these books are
printed in **bold**. Their meanings
are explained in the glossary
on page 30.

Library of Congress Cataloguing-in-Publication Data

Baldwin, Dorothy.
  Health and friends.

  (Your health)
  Bibliography: p.
  Includes index.
  Summary: Discusses the importance of friendships
and examines the elements that make up a successful
friendship.
  1. Friendship — Juvenile literature. [1. Friendship.
2. Interpersonal relations] I. Title. II Series:
Baldwin, Dorothy. Your health.
BF575.F66B35   1987   158′.2   87–13008
ISBN 0–86592–289–6

First published in the
United States in 1987 by
Rourke Enterprises, Inc.
Vero Beach, FL 32964

Typeset by DP Press, Sevenoaks, Kent
Printed in Italy by Sagdos S.p.A. Milan

Contents

Who are you? – Roles

Are you a daughter? Son? Sister? Brother? Cousin? Grandchild? Friend? Neighbor? Pupil? Can you add any other names to this list?

You are you. There is no one else in the world exactly like you. But you also play a part in other people's lives. Within your family you have different **roles** to play. You behave slightly differently within each role. For example, brothers and sisters act differently together from the way they do with their parents or friends. Parents behave differently together from the way they do when they are with their children or friends.

Throughout your life you will play many different roles. Does your behavior change when you are with your family?

4

How do you behave when talking to a neighbor?

Throughout life, each person has many different roles to play.

Your feelings

Do you like yourself? A lot? A little? The way you feel about yourself largely depends on the way you think people feel about you. It also depends on the way you feel about other people. Your feelings are called your **emotions**. They are feelings such as love and hate, joy and sorrow, kindness and cruelty, fairness and spite. Can you name any more? At times, they can be very strong and passionate. At other times, they can be mild. Each person is a mixture of all the emotions. Each **relationship** has a mixture of all the emotions in it.

Do you behave differently when you are with a friend?

Love, liking and understanding

Love can be very passionate and feel very intense. It can also be a milder friendly liking. Love and liking are the emotions that make people happy. On an average, happy people are more healthy than unhappy people. However, each person is capable of feeling many other emotions.

Getting along with people can sometimes cause problems. Not only do you have to think of their feelings, you also have to understand your own. If you have any problems with your relationships, you can learn **skills** to help things go more smoothly. The more you try to get along with people, the happier – and healthier – you are likely to be. Why?

Support

Every now and then, things go wrong for people. They have accidents, fail exams, lose their jobs, feel afraid and so on. When something bad happens, the people become upset, anxious and angry. They need other people to help them get over their painful feelings. They need to cheer up and be happy again as soon as they can.

People who help at those times are said to give their **support**. This is much the same as a prop

Young children show their affection for their friends very easily and openly.

Everybody needs somebody to lean on at times!

that holds up a wall to stop it from falling down. In times of trouble, people who have no support can break down and become **mentally ill**. Without help from other people, they are crushed by unhappy feelings. If the mental pain goes on for too long, they cannot recover on their own.

People tend to get support from their families and friends. In times of trouble, they rush to them for help. Sometimes not much can be done

– you cannot make someone pass an exam if they have failed it. What you can do is to help them to cope with their painful feelings. You listen, you comfort, you soothe, you advise. You make the person feel better. In fact, you act like a true friend.

Friends share their emotions, the good ones and the bad. It would not be fair to use people for support only when you are unhappy. You also share your happy times with them, and you expect them to share their good and bad times with you. The "best" friends are people to whom you can give happy feelings as well as receive them. Love and support starts right from the cradle. It begins with family life.

Giving support *to a friend who has been upset is an important* skill *that will make a friendship stronger.*

The family

Kinship

All the people who are related to you by blood or marriage are your kin and so kinship means "family." Your feelings toward your kin are so strong that they last all through your life. Because each family is different from every other family, there cannot be general "rules" about how kin behave. Families make up their own rules as they go along. However, you may find some of the things that work well with your friends will also work well with your family – see page 20.

Families invent their own rules of behavior.

Older children often welcome the chance to be responsible for feeding a younger brother or sister.

Love begins with your kin. Babies are given love and support from the moment they are born. They are picked up and cuddled. They are fed, washed and played with. Babies do not do anything to get love and support. They just lie back and gurgle happily at all the attention they are receiving.

As the baby grows, things start to change. Small children are taught to look after themselves – to dress, wash and feed themselves. Later, they go to school and have to fit in with everyone else. They stop being the center of attention. This makes some children very unhappy. They sulk or show off to try to bring the attention back on themselves. This is a perfectly natural way to behave when you are still very young.

Give-and-take

The older you are, the more you understand how important love and support are. You learn that to earn them, you have to give them. Kin are incredibly important. They go on loving and supporting you whatever your behavior is like. But other people act differently. They want to know what sort of a person you are before they can start liking you.

Some kin say they are "taken for granted" by their teenage relatives. Do you think that they feel they are not getting back some of the love and support they keep giving? The teens is a time for having close friendships with other teenagers outside the family, but do not forget your kin. Make sure, you are not cutting out your family altogether and making them feel unwanted. People have oceans of love inside them. The more people you love and support, the happier and healthier you can be.

One way of showing your affection for your parents is to remember special occasions and try to give them a treat.

Conflict

During the teens, you and your kin may clash occasionally. The important thing to understand is that **conflict** is quite natural. The closer you are to a person, the stronger your emotions are going to be. Although arguments can make people feel awful, conflict is not always "bad." Learning to cope with conflict at home helps you to cope with it later in life. If you are in conflict with your kin, it does not mean that your home is "bad." Conflict is "bad" only if it goes on and on and people are unhappy all the time.

Sisters and brothers are called **siblings**. According to some studies, in about 71 percent of all families, there are conflicts between siblings. This is called **sibling rivalry**. The rivalry almost always begins when the siblings are very young. Each child wants to be the center of attention and to get all the parents' love. Young children do not know there is plenty of love to go around. They begin quarreling and their conflicts turn into a habit.

In fact, there is love and support between siblings, whether they quarrel or not. It shows when they are grown up and are not rivals for their parents' attention any more. Most siblings love one another deeply, and may sometimes end up sharing a home when they are old. Although you may be in conflict with your sibling now, your relationship will last throughout your life.

Sibling rivalry *is very common in most families.* Siblings *often enjoy a mock fight!*

The lessons learned from earlier sibling conflict *often help you later on when you take part in competitive games.*

Friends

Are you shy? Do you think you have enough friends? Most people have to "earn" their friends. Friendship starts off with liking another person. It can stay that way or it can move to close love. It can suddenly break off, leaving one of the friends feeling very unhappy. Or it can simply fade away as the people grow up, change, or move to another place.

You do not choose your family. But you do choose your friends. If you turn back to page 9, you will read that the "best" friends are those people to whom you can give support knowing that they will give you support in return. Can you work out why? Friends like to share. If one person in the friendship always takes and does not give support, they stop being friends after a while. Without saying anything, they both understand that this is not real sharing. If you have a friendship that has suddenly come to an end, try to work out whether it was because there was not enough sharing.

Self-disclosure

This is a difficult word for something very simple. It means being able to talk about yourself, and "disclose" or uncover your real feelings.

Sometimes, if you have to admit to feelings like cruelty, greed or spite, **self-disclosure** is not easy or pleasant. But remember, these feelings are in everyone. We try to control them; we try to be fair. Often we pretend they are not there because we are ashamed of them or because they frighten us. By disclosing your true feelings to somebody else, you accept them and they stop feeling so frightening. You can even get pleasure from the way you are coping with them.

It is not just the bad feelings that are hard to disclose. Feelings like love and joy can be difficult too. But, if you are happy, you can spread happiness by sharing it.

Sharing your worries with a sympathetic older person can do a great deal to ease your mind.

Girls often find self-disclosure easier than boys. Boys used to be trained not to think too deeply about themselves. Being able to talk about yourself often depends on how close you are to members of your family. You can choose whether you want to talk about your inner feelings or not. It is one of the skills of having friends. You support your friends through their unhappy feelings, and you get the same kind of support back.

Empathy

Empathy is another kind of role you take on. It is like **sympathy** and is an important skill between friends. It can be learned.

Do you ever empathize *with the experiences of a character in a story as these children are doing?*

When you feel sympathy, this means that you understand a friend's problem and that you are sorry for him or her. Empathy means sympathy, but it means something much deeper too. You imagine that you can actually feel the same emotions as your friend, that you are your friend. You are able to feel the same happy or unhappy things your friend feels. People often say that they empathize with the feelings of characters in books and films too.

It is easy to sympathize with a friend. It is just as easy to empathize too. However, you can sympathize without feeling any pain. When you empathize, you take on the painful feelings as well. This is not likely to make you happy! You may have enough of your own painful feelings without taking on any more. And there will be times when you find it impossible to empathize because you cannot imagine what it feels like to be your friend.

As with self-disclosure, you can choose to feel your friend's pain, or not. There are times when it is not wise. Nurses would not be good at their work if they felt all their patients' pain. We expect them to sympathize, not empathize. It is not wise to empathize on those days when you think it will make you too unhappy yourself. You will become useless as a friend. An important part of providing support is to cheer your friend up. You cannot do this if you have become too miserable yourself.

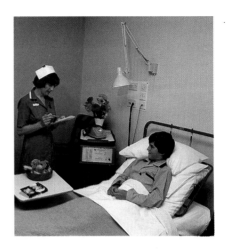

Nurses and doctors must not allow themselves to empathize with their patients when they are in pain because it would make their jobs more difficult.

Young people often suffer from painful shyness, which stops them from mixing with large groups of people. What do you think are the best ways to combat shyness?

How many friends do you have?

Do you have a lot of friends? A few? None? During the teens, people worry about being popular. The person who is always in the center of a crowd is the envy of everyone else. In fact, being popular is not as important as it seems. Popular people often do not have real friends. They have **acquaintances**, people they need for company, but nothing else. A friend is someone who is very close and shares the things that are most important of all – your feelings and theirs.

A recent study found that many young people are lonely. Some young people feel lonely even in the middle of a crowd. Try not to worry whether you are popular or not. One real friend is worth hundreds of acquaintances. Keep remembering that you will be happier – and healthier – with one person who is important in your life. You have to work hard to make and keep a friend, but most of the good things in life only come with hard work.

Loyalty and trust

To make a friendship work, there are "rules" that both people must not break. These rules are not written down. They are rarely spoken aloud.

Loyalty and trust are two of the most important ingredients of a good friendship, when friends can share their deepest thoughts without fear of being teased or having their trust betrayed. These girls in their middle teens have learned how important this is.

Do you think loyalty and trust are two of the most important things? If you do, can you understand the reasons why?

When you tell a friend the secret "bad" bits about yourself, you are **vulnerable**. Your emotions are at risk. If something goes wrong in the friendship, your friend can give your secrets away or tease you about them. There is a chance that this will upset you and that you will do the same thing in return. People who are lonely may have had their feelings hurt in this way in the past. The pain of what happened then goes on and on, and stops them from wanting to try to make new friends.

It is important for people to make eye contact so that they can see each other's reactions.

You can do a lot of harm to a friendship by sulking and refusing to tell a friend what is wrong.

Some rules of friendship

SOME "RULES"

1. Keep secrets.
2. Wait for your friend to offer secrets; do not pry.
3. Share your happy times as well as your sad times.
4. Stand up for your friend.
5. Show loving support.
6. Ask your friend for support when you need help.
7. Offer help; do not wait for your friend to ask.
8. Make sure you return borrowed things.
9. If your friend hurts your feelings, say so. Do not go off in a sulk.
10. Look in your friend's eyes when you talk.
11. Do not joke or tease your friend.
12. Do not be jealous of your friend's other relationships, especially with their kin.

Do you agree with most things on the list? Would you like to add some more of your own? The list came from a survey of what people wanted from their friends. Which three "rules" do you think are most important?

Read rule 9 once again. Friends can hurt each other's feelings without meaning to. If one person goes away in a sulk, the other person has

Share the happy moments with your friends, not just the sad ones.

no idea what has gone wrong. A really good friendship can be lost if people do not explain what has gone wrong. You need to give a friend the chance to say sorry, and to put things right.

When you break any of these "rules," try not to feel too angry or upset. And try not to feel too hurt if someone has broken the rules against you. It takes time to learn how to make and keep friends. While you are learning, you are likely to make some mistakes. Forgive yourself when you make mistakes. Be ready to forgive your friend's mistakes too.

The main reasons why friendships are lost are because of breaking the rules 1, 7 and 12. Can you figure out which "rules" might be helpful for getting along with your kin? For example, do you always look your kin straight in the eyes when you talk?

Feeling shy

Many young people go through a period of feeling very shy. They become anxious about the way they are growing from children into adults. They worry over their looks, their height, their weight, their strength, their hair, their pimples, their clothes and so on. The more they worry, the more unsure of themselves they become. The more unsure a person feels, the worse the pain of shyness grows. People are not sure how to behave, or whether other people will accept them.

Young people sometimes worry that they are totally unattractive. Self-criticism is very negative. *Try to think* positively *about yourself.*

● Shyness stops people from trying to make friends.

● Shyness stops people from feeling happy about themselves.

● Shyness makes some people show off to cover up their painful feelings.

● Shyness makes other people become too quiet for the same reason.

Shyness is so usual in the teens it is almost a natural feeling. You can take some comfort in knowing that more people suffer from it than you think. It does not happen just because you are anxious about your looks. It also comes from the feeling of not knowing who you really are. The teens is the time for having all sorts of exciting dreams. You long to be famous, to be loved, to be wildly successful in your future life. Try not to spend too much time on your dreams. Lovely though they are, you will need to work hard to make them come true. Dreams can be such a comfort that there is a chance that you will forget about the hard work. You can take refuge in them and forget that one thing you must do is try to cope with feeling shy.

Dreaming your life away may be very pleasurable, but working hard to achieve your aims, or making new friends is more satisfactory in the end.

Comparisons with other people

"I am not as popular, witty, clever or as good at sports as everyone else in my class." Perhaps you are not. But there will be a few things you are: fairly good at, just as good at, even better at than anyone else. Try to reduce the number of

Try to join in group activities, when you can. This will give you less time to ponder over what you see as faults in yourself and let you concentrate on your strengths. It will also make you think of others.

times you compare yourself with other people. It is boring, and it does not help you feel happy. In fact, it can make you feel very sad and your shyness will become even worse. Read the first sentence of this section again. These are called **negative comparisons**. They have to do with what you are not. They are very harsh judgments against yourself.

If you want to compare yourself with others, why not make kind judgments? Making a list of all the things you are good at is a good way to cheer yourself up. These are **positive comparisons**. Or, and better still, you could try not to make comparisons at all. They are not very helpful. Why spend time making yourself miserable, when you could be having fun with a friend? If you can manage to stop making comparisons, the reasons for some of your shyness will simply melt away.

Body language

Your body and its actions "speak" to other people. It gives your feelings away. Look at the picture. Which person is feeling happy? Which is feeling cross? Which is feeling shy? If you wanted to be friends with one of these people, whom would you choose?

Which figure is happy? Which is cross and which is shy? Being aware of body language can help you with other people.

Your body cannot lie. The way you move your body tells the truth about your feelings. This is because body movement and emotions are very closely linked. Sit up straight. Raise your head high. How do you feel? Slump into the chair. Drop your head down. How do you feel? Your body and mind work together to show your feelings.

Study the picture on page 26. Jane (on the right) is doing all the right things to make a friend. Jane is facing Susan. She is smiling, and looking straight into Susan's eyes. She has

Jane (on the right) is signaling to Susan through body language that she wants to be friends.

lowered her book so that it does not form a barrier between herself and Susan.

Looking at the picture of Jane and Susan, can you imagine what people should not do if they want to make a new friend? Often shyness can make people appear awkward and unfriendly.

● They should not turn away, but face another person openly.
● They should not avoid eye contact.
● They should not hold up barriers in the shape of a book or bag.

Practice your body language in a mirror. However shy you feel, try to hold your head up and smile when you want to make a new friend. You will not be able to remember all the other things your body is "saying," so do not worry over them at first. Keep checking that you are smiling and raising your head. Even if it does not always work for other people, it makes you feel less shy and more cheerful about yourself.

A warm, open smile will always attract other people.

No friends?

Not everyone needs friends. Some people have so many kin and are so busy with their family life that there is no time left for friends. Other people have been made so unhappy by people in the past that they do not want to risk making friends again. If you are a popular person, this does not mean that you are "better" than people without any friends. If you are a lonely person, this does not mean that you are "better" because you can manage without any friends.

Sometimes, lonely people comfort themselves by pretending they do not need a friend. There is nothing wrong in that. However, they need to make sure that they are not using this excuse just as a way of avoiding all the hard work that must be put into a good friendship to make it work. In the same way, people who only dream about great futures for themselves avoid working hard to make them come about. Dreams and excuses are comforting, but why spend time comforting yourself when you could be working hard to find a new friend?

Learning from others

You can learn a lot about friendship by watching closely the way people behave. An

Some people prefer to be on their own, and are happy without close friends. If you prefer your own company make sure that this is not because of shyness or because you are not willing to work at your friendships.

even better way is to talk to your family. Ask them if they had any problems when they were your age. Find out if their teenage friendships lasted or not. People enjoy talking about friends from the past. Always remember too, that you can learn a great deal more from older kin than you can from friends of your own age.

Another survey asked young adults who were their best friends. Almost 50 percent of the women said their mother was now their best friend of all!

(Above) *In the same way that you take pleasure in and work hard at a hobby, you must work at your friendships. You will find that sharing hobbies is often a basis for friendship.*

(Left) *Having good relationships with other people, whether family or friends, will improve your sense of well-being.*

Glossary

Acquaintances People with whom we might spend time but whom we do not know well enough to call friends.

Body language The way we move our bodies, the way we sit or stand, can give away something about our inner feelings without us having to speak.

Conflict A clash between two or more people. Sometimes we have conflicting feelings such as wanting to laugh and cry at the same time.

Emotions Feelings, such as love, kindness, jealousy and joy. They can be very strong or quite mild. During the teens, when the body is changing from a child's shape into an adult's, feelings can change very rapidly and suddenly within a short space of time. This is very confusing. Learning to cope with these **emotions** is a sign of growing up.

Empathy Being able to understand another person's feelings so strongly that you can imagine you are feeling those **emotions** yourself.

Mentally ill This means that the mind is ill – that it can no longer cope with everyday life. People who have worn out their minds with long periods of worry become **mentally ill**. (The cure is usually a long rest and medicines.) That is why you should always tell your family and friends about anything that worries you a great deal.

Negative comparisons You make these if you say something is not as good as something else.

Positive comparisons You make these if you say something is as good as or better than something else.

Relationship The way people get along together. There can be friendly **relationships**, working **relationships** or loving **relationships**, for example.

Roles The different ways we behave in certain situations and with certain people.

Self-disclosure Talking about your inner feelings to another person.

Sibling rivalry The clash between brothers and sisters that takes place from an early age and becomes a habit. Children are usually vying for their parents' affection.

Siblings Brothers and sisters.

Skills Ways to behave that will make situations easier. These can be learned.

Support To prop up, to give help when it is needed.

Sympathy Feeling sorry for someone else's problems.

Vulnerable Capable of being hurt, either physically or emotionally.

Further reading

If you would like to read more about this subject, you may find these books useful:

Booher, Dianna Daniels, *Making Friends With Yourself & Other Strangers.* Messner, 1982.

LeShan, Eda, *You And Your Feelings.* Macmillan, 1975.

Naylor, Phyllis Reynolds, *Getting Along With Your Friends.* Abingdon, 1980.

Richards, Arlene Kramer, *Boy Friends, Girl Friends, Just Friends.* Atheneum, 1979.

Varenhorst, Barbarba B., *Real Friends: Becoming The Friend You'd Like To Have.* Harper, 1983.

Reading Ladders For Human Relations. National Council of Teachers of English, 1981.

Picture acknowledgments

The Publisher would like to thank the following for providing pictures for the book: Ace Photo Agency 16, 17, 19 (Martin Riedl), 29 (right); Ann Baum 22, 25; Ed Carr 8; Tim Humphrey 4, 5, 6, 9, 15, 18, 20 (below), 21, 26, 27, 28; Orpix 20 (above); Vision International – Anthea Sieveking 7, 10, 11, 23, 24 – R. Parker 13 (below); Tim Woodcock cover; Zefa 29 (left).

Index